MAP OF THE
FOLDED WORLD

D0872989

AKRON SERIES IN POETRY

MAP
OF THE
FOLDED
WORLD

Poems by

JOHN GALLAHER

The University of Akron Press
Akron, Ohio

13   12   11   10   09   5   4   3   2   1

LIBRARY OF CONGRESS CATALOGING-IN-PUBLICATION DATA
Gallaher, John, 1965-
  Map of the folded world / John Gallaher. —1st ed.
    p. cm. — (Akron series in poetry)
  ISBN 978-1-931968-62-1 (pbk. : alk. paper)
  I. Title.
  PS3607.A415M37 2009
  811'.6—DC22
                        2008053226

Cover: "An Abundance of Caution," Acrylic on paper, Amy Casey, 2008.
Part pages: "Stacked," Acrylic on paper, Amy Casey, 2007.

Contents

one

two

three

There are known knowns. There are things we know that we know. There are known unknowns. That is to say, there are things that we now know we don't know. But there are also unknown unknowns. There are things we do not know we don't know.

—*Donald Rumsfeld, 2002*

one

Watermelon in the Afternoon

Several grandmothers are in a half-circle
eating watermelon from plastic cups.

Let us not forget to act differently.
Let us not forget
to start the music, to play the music loud.

And stir the chairs as they empty.
And close the rooms.

Call the families, then. The several families
down the hall.

Go tell the skinny girls.

The trees are up against the windows.
The wind is up against the trees. And everyone lies down
where they fall.

And this other part, where we think only
watermelon, only
flaring color.

Who knows you should have had
more sense?

Who knows there is more sense?

Earth-tone Anecdote

They are speaking in the other room,
about the family. They are speaking,
and weren't the families over,
and roiling. Didn't the families take off
and return, and in returning,
take off—

These were the first stories told me.
And wasn't I harder then, more
demanding,
in need of explicating.

Wasn't it something for the mind
at the top of the stairs, where the children sit,
listening.

In the doorways they bend behind,
didn't the families sound like crumpling paper,
like cedar in the fireplace,
and the white doors to the kitchen.

Weren't all the doors open then,
to the yard, to the trees this way
in the wind.

Didn't their singing please you.

And isn't pleasing something only seasons do.
A bit of wind in the trees.

They are closing the windows. They are
speaking in the other room,
about the family.

Weren't the children up
and flying
about the chandelier.

Didn't they find the chimney
and go.

The Danger in Plans

If you are just funny enough,
if you can just run fast enough,
no one will ever die.

Do you remember that?
And are you better now?

And all our meaning statements.
All our looking at things.

The women laughing around the table
in the kitchen.

Trouble on the way, and great joy.

I'm okay with it, but who's to know
the way I might feel
back then.
The men standing in the yard,
talking and laughing.

You forgot to watch me close my beautiful eyes,
the unspeaking gods
in a row,
at the edge of anything, toward.

The music of that.
The becoming. And maybe you are there.

Maybe you have ten coins.

The Way We Live Now

I told as much of the truth as I could imagine.
And something about the largeness of water, with your bridge of
    orange and your bridge of sandalwood.
And the oceans sloshing at the trees.
With the meek bridges and the splendid bridges.
Look, everyone is out on all the bridges, to and back.
Connectivity, they're saying, so small.
And I have this argument to make.
Forth then, and fro.
And each shore is the shore.
And each shore is the last flight out.
The press of bodies slowed us to a near stop.
Did you see my rapid leg just then, or the other one?
When we all got to the end of grammar and began to float.
It was only tall and taller.
And then your bridges were somehow gone.
The train and the kissing bridges.
The sad and silver bridges to stand on all night.
And we all shared one thought.
One crowded thought.

What We're Up Against

On the way home from the funeral
we stopped for lunch.

Lunch was like the singing. Lunch
was like the flowers. The hole,

where we all began standing around
each other's buildings, eating,

and bringing more buildings with us.

When the air started thinning,
we sang that living was like this. We sang
for the ambulance

in front of the house. We waved.

The doctors stood around
mumbling
and checking off racing forms.

You breathed out and out
over the back wall you made
out of Coke bottles.

Someone in the other room
was playing a piano.

What are we going to do now,
we asked, placing sandwiches

in front of the empty seat
over and over,

until that's all there was.

On the Map of the Folded World

We're at a great distance.
Little specks of things.

We have this hunger.

So let us contemplate the hand. The distance
of the hand.
The grasping of the distance.
The hollow of the eye.

Let us say we are walking into a building
we'll not walk out of.

We know we're all here
somewhere. The table is set.
There are plants along the window.

Out of curiosity. Out of the body
travel.

We consist of smaller things.
"The curtains kept swaying."

We'll tell each other about it.
We'll accuse each other of not caring enough
about what we care about.

As we're all folding
from our houses. Folding into the yards.

Our flaming streets. Our streets
in flame.

Keys to Successful Disappearing

The statues are congregating in the courtyard,
and the dolls are all staring at us. We're running about.

We're laughing in the shrubbery. What were we, anyway,
sixteen or so? Jenny

asks. We must've been visiting someplace
important. I think it was the house

of an ex-president. And then we were reminded that alcohol
is a toxin. Roosevelt maybe, or Jefferson,

mounted under the shelf. Just to stand there (*shhh!*)
and to keep standing there, the room

doing flippy-flops. And not to be saying anything.
Nothing, really. And Buffy and Bucky, almost, out

in the field house. This's the old geography,
Mr. Cartouches said, organized and out-of-the-

way, yet totally accessible. Jenny touches the mirror. Waves.
What an atrium, we thought, and this

embossed mirror to keep it all in place.

I wish I could remember where that was,
and had a set of directions.

When One Has Lived Too Long
Among Other People

Because life is a puzzle
isn't it, there is a person framed
by a window, stuck
on repeat.

Once they carried the entertaining
sunset around. Look, isn't this
entertaining?

And look, isn't it your body
that does the dreaming, the settled sunsets
stuck on repeat?

I am writing a note, I am not
falling down. I am writing X
of windows. I am thinking
there is no more.

That these are larger boxes
in this city, stuck on repeat.

We call it the apology of.
Or we call it the apothecary
landscape of.

I'm standing in a hospital room,
dusting you, for days.

If everything could only be cleaner.

When one has spent a long time
among others, the windows
are these little windows.

Here is a flower stuck on repeat,
to cross the summer rooms, to write
the summer notes.

The Rejected House

Strangers arrive with their old lovers in town
for the weekend. None of us
has ever had it so good. The shelves are full
of rubber fruit. Teeming, we say.
There's a television on. It's a tennis match.
Someone's whispering *love*
into a cell phone. The person on the other end
is asking
for pictures of this house
that was rejected
for being a surface house, a distant house.

"Look," Margo says, "I'm made of glass
and covered in glass." And the yard is full
of chickens' blood
and pianos on fire. And the chickens are full
of the blood of yards
as vans full of illegal workers pass
with pickups full of illegal workers
throwing each other into the ocean
many miles away
where we hear there are no oceans.

Many miles away, I'm holding the house
over the flower bed, so my desperation
can have an easier view
of another summer of birds
falling from the sky
onto this house that starts and stops. This house
that turns slowly above me in the breeze.

Why did I never realize
the house was so light, was this light?
Can this really be what all the fuss was about?
Just something with a little blood on it?

Apostrophe to the Dead

Hello, dear wasting-your-heart-there, dear
imaginary friend. The oak has moved
over the roof line.
It's what distance is for,

with all these scraps of paper
and so little to say
over a headache and coffee.

Come back for an hour.
I've been thinking
of bringing the gods home,
of singing the gods to sleep.

Here with only the sorts of things
I can conceptualize,
no longer watching the details,
however much they matter,
which goes missing
in the scenery.

The robins following
the lawnmower, the robins
at the edge of the sprinkler's arc.

And here I am. And here we are.
In the falling apart house.
In the falling apart body.

Disguised Afternoon

All the old people left and then we were the old people.
And the weather rolling in.
We were having no luck
getting our kites up in the air. But we didn't mind.
We kept our doubts to ourselves.

On their way home, the friends passed a meadow
filled with flowers.
And the trees beyond the houses.
There were tulips and daisies and daffodils.

Your idea got me to thinking
just then. All the things
that were duration, perhaps they're floating away
in a bubble
out over a cliff face and river.

And there are boats in the river.
And people in the boats.

The big smiles, and the pillow
of those days
in our turn (the grass & hills), as the people circling
are the circling people

all around you
from where you are.

This in Which Guidebook

Shh, close your eyes.
Shh, close your eyes
just for a second. I have some good news
and some bad news.

The family is singing downstairs.
It's a drama. We're acting.

Why don't you sing with your pretty voice.
Why don't you dance
from wall to wall.

I am not dumb.

We're saying, *You be the parents
now.* Or, *You be the walls.* Or, *Happy
New Year.* Or, *I've had this much wine.*

The rain will make less noise.

And the walls will say I have not been good
     enough
to everyone. And I will say,
No, I have not.

The family will say, *This is salt,
and this is pepper.*

What you need to know.

And you get to be the monkey in the middle.
And you get a telephone.
And you get to hear it ring.

The plants are very large on the patio.
Where we spy each other out.
Where we close our eyes.

It's Any Move. It's That People Are Places.

Things, not emotions.
Where you're falling off a corner
into the sea.
The many boats.

Or the picture of skin over your bones.
The better picture.

We drove to the coast and it took three days.
We stood in the water.

What unquestionable good news. Where the life
and the dream of the life
are one.

The square of the blanket and the blankets in squares.
Such an ordinary place.
The umbrellas in circles.

Which turns into a chase around town
for everyone.

There is this family
like wind through the umbrellas.
There are these palms
in the wind.

Here's a boat with water in it.

The water has a hole in it,
where we've been and where we've not been,
reenacting the scene
without sound.

What & Who & Where & What

Decorative treatment of surface and space.
And I'm right here at the window or the door looking at the standing wave.
The two figures in a choreographed dance.
The house and the yard.
It's a nice time.
A bit of light, and my personal symbolism of everyday objects.
The spoon against the bowl, for instance.
The window against the wall.
Sharp linearity, order, and balance.
And this father in a car off a bridge.
And this brother who forgot to keep breathing some Monday afternoon on
    the back porch.
The car on the shelf.
The afternoon.
There may be no single answer, and these sleek, impersonal surfaces.
The chair.
The nude on the wall.
In the room of the dead, you're stomping around again.
You'll never be quiet.
In the solid blocks of color that form a backdrop to the scene, presenting
    itself.
And which father are you there, the dead one or the one dying?
Blue and green.
Or blue and white and light blue and blue and green and yellow and olive.
But these are suggestions, not depictions.
There's the sound of the ocean, or traffic.

Fetish for the World Without Memory

The dark shade of the house,
the house's twin, the night's other, is cool
and just fine. And then
tomorrow's episode.

The thing surrounded
by the conception of the thing.

We had some questions, and then realized
quite a bit of time had gone by
with no questions.

Standing in the yard, imagining it
just that way. Looking at the blue sky
imagining blue sky.

Maybe in June. Maybe
thinking *June*. We might as well call these things
true happenings, as history goes
to the stubborn story,
and any random version of yourself
might become what you're known by.

The green of those green days.
The house in shade. Where your father goes.
And your mother goes.

I will walk under those clouds
and I will breathe that air
in the amnesia city in the country of amnesia.

Unfathom me. Turn me inside out.
Thin as that. Thinner.

Poem for the End of January

In the wind, the so-much wind,
call them a couple people in winter,
dark against the snow.

What has who they are to do with it,
this winter wind,
this calling them?

What has who we imagine them to be
to do with it,
in the elocution of the wind,

to speak the countable trees up and down
in a glaze of snow over ice,
without sanctuary?

As seeing is further surfaces.
And when it is done,
we all have new names.

What has winter to do with it?
What has the wind
to do with it?

This performance in pale hues.
Some calendar photograph. Some figures
in morning snow.

Which is dark against light. Which is
that I don't mean any of this.
It's winter. I'm reading from the script.

two

Anecdote of the Disappearances

I'm standing in one of the upper rooms,
at night,
the weather making progress at the window.

It is deep spring.

I'm standing in one of the yards,
my lover past a window.

The window is dark. My lover
rises from a lake
and recedes.

I'm counting houses,
starting with small numbers. I'm saying, one,
followed by one.

My lover says the Christmas cactus
is falling apart.
Magazines from florists
cover the coffee table around it.

My lover is holding knives.

I'm standing for a photograph. The photographs
are rising from a lake.

We're going to go swimming. We swim.

It is deep spring.

We're playing with the invisible children.
We're racing.

American Rivers

On the perfect surface, our houses will fail. This hole
that is the ceiling
where we'll sit, eating what we have. This edge
where we'll swing our feet.

The distance to the ground
where we'll be feasting
or disappearing. Where the bank fails.

We sing. We sing
to the air across the rivers, where we file in rows,
past Kansas City and Des Moines.

The stars will start talking again.
We'll have carts, and what we can carry.
We'll have our apologies.

I can count the rivers of America
this way. I can count the rivers
that flow from south to north, and I can count everyone
in this room.

We say we already know, after dinner,
laughing at the roof.
We'll call someone tomorrow. We go outside.

We draw across the stars
in straight lines.

We'll carry all that we can carry. We'll have sex
by the roadside.

I'll tell you what I want you to say.
I want you to say there's a mathematics to this.

I want you to say it
as you take off your clothes.

Minneapolis Is a Fine City

Or maybe you love me and then you don't,
or never did, or I you,
and I quietly lose your name
among the bridges and news.

Up and down the corridors,
grabbing things from filing cabinets,

or hearing people up and off the diving boards,
the sharp then dull cha-chunk up
and then the water
as what the water always does. The radio and people.

Hello and hello to you too. Perhaps
a margarita, or something
alone under its umbrella. Red maybe,

or pink. Your gradations a pale form
of a woman in love. Or fourteen people by the pool
in love with eleven people
with some overlap.
And overlap as a spectator sport, and
spectators as a form of eclipse,
eclipse as a wet bar of sorrow, and all these other ways
no one feels special
on which we hadn't counted.

Because it's all you can know.
Because it's all you can touch. Here

are your enigmatic draperies.
Here are your pejorative sunsets.

And so why be a body at all?
Why be anything?

Close, or Somewhat Close

We could hear the music long before
we could place it, and fold into diagrams of rooms
we once thought were large as the things now
that pass for fruitless telephone calls
we hope no one remembers
we swore we'd never make.

Duck Duck Goose we called it in simpler times,
until we realized it meant funerals
and a constant supply of dry cleaning.
But were there ever really simpler times?
And what shall I do now, as the hand
is going from forehead to forehead,
and all I can think
is how you looked in the kitchen chair
with my hand moving down your zipper.

The trees, so near to touching you,
you can barely stand it.
It was all right with me. I'm not territorial, as I watch
and keep watching
you walk away. Watch, you say, wouldn't you
like me? Well, yes, sure, but what about the rest
of the night? And what about the ducks
and their row? What about the chickens?

It's a long walk.
I've plenty of time to think.

Isn't life funny, the guests all said. Yes, and
isn't it funny, too, what you say
when no one is listening, and you're wearing that outfit.
You know the one, the one
you refused to describe to me
while the city drowned in feathers.

It really doesn't matter, though, what
you're drowning in,
once you realize you're drowning.

& All Things Repeatingly

And these people fill my thoughts.
Girl in a bottle.
Girl in the woods.
My baby's asleep and my other baby's asleep.
In the drama, an oboe felled the trees.
I meant to say *filled*, lovers dashed in the trees.
And I will sit on this roof, becoming the picture.
The black road and white trees.
The long lines and bright trees.
The long thin lines.
We will do nobody any good.
A gentle breeze is blowing. The frame flutters.
Girl in negative.
Girl in a glaze of language, approaching to a spot.
Throwing ourselves at each other.
Placing ourselves.
And then approaching to a spot.
We could just keep standing here, and continue vanishing.
If only to see things we know.
I'm sitting at a table.
I'm counting on my fingers and my toes.

Anecdote of the Little Houses

They're folding maps out across the yards,
over the houses
on the north side of the street
and on the south.

Look, darling, they say, *the houses
are all lit up.*
It's a summer night, in blue.

In the houses, they've gotten new clothes
and they're trying them on.
They're saying *yes*,

and they're saying *no*,
whenever they step from a room.
They're saying, *I think so*, and *is*, or *isn't*.

The people
are folding maps out
across the streets.

Time keeps running out, they say,
and there keeps being more of it
as the surfaces flash by.

And below,
after they stop at their houses,
the lines rise above the lines.

The red and the blue lines
rising and falling all night
in their sleep.

More Versions of
It's Real If You Say It Is

The color of your eyes.
The distance of the field.

And the field in the distance
full of people.

We made it through the city,
or through the lights
of the city.

I'll try not to worry you, we say,
watching the parks. I'll try not
to be anything or move anything.

It's what the country does. What
the year. The house I keep driving past
for no other reason.

Because if you keep coming back,
maybe everything
comes back
for your little green hat,
as you're surrounded in falling leaves
some November. Some
October, so full of driving past the fields,
only movement is real.

Only the body on top
of the body. The body riding the body.

And sometimes we say things
only because they sound good,
when you think perhaps it's building to something,
and then that's all there is.

But don't let it worry you.

When you go clear,
and the streetlights are passing,
we're all going clear.

Caution to the Wind

It's somewhere there in your big book
of spy rules, that maybe you'll never know who did
and who didn't, and you'll have to deal with not knowing,
waiting out in the car with the radio on
and another of the things everyone does bit by bit,
watching the show go by.

What was that trying to cross the road? And why?
As the other side is just the same as this one,
even if they never meet, though they're famous for their optimism
that one day they will. It's another of the ways we pay,
like leaving the possibility of bad news
for no news at all, which often
doesn't sound like such a bad deal,
when you ignore yourself
and stop for billboards.

And then there's this other trick, though maybe with some clues
sprinkled around, which is the promise of all tricks,
isn't it? Some edge of a clue? The way you know what I'm saying already,
as you've been here and been here, several times,
the weather always about to change, and it's late,
and you've named it your way
several layers down, across a heaven of surfaces.

Perhaps there's comfort in that
for someone, or a more subtle joke
that sounds like the paint failing and lamentations
all up and down the city streets,
and it's test day, right? And no one told you how,
or where, or to what purpose.

You're thinking maybe you really should have kept looking,
and never stopped.
And how you should be looking now.
The afternoon is enormous
as it lumbers across the empty lawns to the sea.

With the Sunset Machine

The door is open. The door
is closed. The chorus of the self
dressing up in little outfits.

The chorus of the self on the road,
taking a little trip. Bright trees,
where one can foster all manner
of afternoons, and counter-
afternoons, driving.

Where one can lament
the trailing of the idea, amid fewer thoughts
and comfortable scenery.

And glib weather. And extravagant
forecasts. Which turned out to be
what we thought they were,
though we didn't know that then,
expectations being what they are.

It's the way mystery works.

And the inevitable death-bed conversions,
shamed into it, or divided
from ourselves.

There are so many ways to step into the future.

The chorus of the self with the moral mask
or the circus mask, a bit older
and then a bit older after that,

taking a little trip.
The trailing of the idea.

For All Things Going Eventually

Long past the last afternoon in your living room. Dark fetish.
And some nice, fixed notions of things.
Like the only thing a fool will never forget is being called a fool.
And a cup of good cheer, rising like Texas. Horizon fetish.
Which leaves a little window open for no regret. Doe-eyed fetish.
I just came to ask you a question.
Time has passed, and things are different from what they were.
Fetish of our bodies intertwined.
Fetish of buried houses. Limping fetish.
Let's not make a production of it, in our loose days, at that moment
        everything they say about you comes true. Fetish of windows.
Such intimacies.
Setting the furniture up in rows across the lawns. Taking our places.
        Setting the lawns in rows.
Fetish of any back room where I'm losing this town.
I'm losing my left eye. Fetish of forgetting.
And when the time is up, everyone leaves.
Fetish of stealing away, like some large, deficient bird.

Girl Playing with Toy Soldiers

They're going to the store. They need things.
It's late. It's almost six o'clock.

They have to take a bath later,
and will they float?

Will they float
in the shape of the house,
the black and white house?

Later, we'll clean the patio
and we'll get a silver star.

Later, in a photograph of the patio,
where I'm almost walking
like I used to.

My hands across the walls. My hand
across my cheek.

This is my testimony.

In this other world,
it's the resistant surface
that makes me stand there,
watching the air,
and the false color of that. The false picture

of a girl in the woods sleeping.

Your Golden Ticket

It will be your greatest moment,
your zenith, your heart.

Bicycles left in the yard, glistening in dew
and so much depending, sing it.

And the squirrels hear it, falling from the trees,
they hear it.

This is your moment.

Tickets taken,
tickets ripped in pieces, your golden ticket
blowing across the yard.

How many flashes? How many
cars of girls?

The people gathering from their houses
into the streets. The mailboxes flapping.
Satellite dishes spinning.

All these people
approaching this great moment. Your moment.

You know the secret language.

You can hear it
between the oak and the sycamore,
the truck and the road,
the black heart of sky dancing through you.

Pardon Me for Asking

You always looked better that way. Saying,
no. Saying, *I'm feeling sassy tonight.*

It was lovely, though, wasn't it? When you got to the part
about ordering drinks, and we both talked
at once, and laughed, and then said, *no, you,*
and then we both talked at once,
and began weeping, though no one ever knew why,
least of all us, and suddenly it's all a matter
of finding the quickest way
somewhere else, sleeping late. And later.

And even if it was, well, what then? What
are you going to do with so many conversations
about how conversations should go?

Paint the road from there to here
for instance, in the shape of a narrowing V. And the bottles of light
across the counter. The bottles of French air.
The only thing we're sure of
is that surety is called for. Maybe that's enough?

And I've never been good with people looking better
that way. Or upset people. Or people
I really wanted to meet, or otherwise touch,
but only in the evenings
when the cicadas were a bit of genius
the director thought up, whether or if
there ever was a director
or any thinking involved.

Isn't it just magic? Isn't it just another wondrous box
you can't wait to hold and hold and hold
and never open again?

Public Afternoon

These people are mad at these people.
This woman is mad at her mother.
Her kids are too old for this Easter stuff.

They were treated for minor injuries and released.
What we call minor.
And your reading of it.
What is your reading of it.

Maybe a dog would help.
This dog is not the dog.
What we call inner.

That's a big house.
Maybe the cartoons live there.
That's a tiny house.
Tiny people must live in it.

There was a small shop there.
Everything is moving. It must be alive.
We are speaking for what color.

Where my hands shake a bit, signaling something to those
        there waiting for a signal.
The signal's blue, or evening.
Dog or cloud.

Therefore the grass, the small plants.

The Street

You can chase the red ball, or, in the black dress,
you can put out your right hand
so that it looks as if you're touching something
other than air.

On the street, you can shoulder a two-by-eight
in your delivery suit
past the anonymous lover
the young woman wants rid of. The hand
is a salute, isn't it? If you're the one
crossing your chest, or the one pointing to the red ball.

The young woman wishes to be anywhere else
but in his grasp, upon the sidewalk maybe,
or as a child, while the child wishes to be anyone else
but shrunken, and carried away.

You can stare away from here, in your chef hat,
on this street of blank signs
and no clutter,
and say, there is a ball, or a hoop
and a ball.

Work for Killing Time

In the company of others, we work.
We work these hills into mountains, rivers into mountains, mountains
    into marking time.
Into crossing the mountains.
The trees will be cut.
The rivers will be cut.
The counting of clouds will be spring and snowmelt.
I am full today of coffee and bringing-forth.
What you said that afternoon was what the rocks are being made to say. This
    road.
This kingdom of roads.
There, look at the way the hill is ringed, the river is ringed, the desert is folded
    into towers.
We work in the company of events in time.
We have roads, the right of the road, and the left of the road.
And the earth is not touched.
And the earth under the earth is not touched.
It will be revealed in a deeper eroding.
In a harsher, more devastating renewal.

three

The Glitter Caught You

The night sounded all hollow and rushing,
and then these mysterious carpet burns that make delicious ovals,
halfway to drawing faces on ourselves
while they keep telling us things we've done
that we don't remember doing
or contemplating, but we do, and contemplate doing
so many things
above the lake or after a night at the restaurant,
where the tablecloths keep waving
in their whiteness, and we have so little left by the end,
it hardly seems like the end
or a white flag in the parking lot
and the reviews trickling in, though the admission was free
and no one is who they were
past the beautiful feel of their skin
and their moment there, their only moment
of no wishing, and nothing left
past the kinds of sounds clouds make, or your fingers
through the clouds, when there are no clouds, and it's night,
or it could be night,
and we're finally kind of wonderful in our way.

Three Panels in Praise of Damage Control

Built up into this large thing,
it certainly might look like it means something,
but then what? We might get to thinking there's anything special
about ourselves, or wait, what did I mean again? Look,
the fields are in bloom, and the deer are peeking out,
looking for the garden one more time.

The town is closing up for the night, helpless as a garden,
or as the unforeseen responses people occasion. Something
you have to believe your way into, which is enough
to collect coins or to help a baby lamb find its mother
two thirds of the way through the story,
until they have to open up a brand new category
and call it "lovers in the trees," where everybody's good
and it's a constant joy, if a bit of a blur
and later some falling down
and carrying back to the car.

When I find I don't know what to say or do,
I've decided I should thank someone. So thank you then,
and thank you to the deer at the tree line,
and the several streets one might walk down at any hour of the night,
and all the stars one might count, with a helpful hand or two
in case you should stumble.

And then panel three, which is always a falling off, saying, "Look,
I'm falling off, I know, but I'm tired
of great art, or even good art.
It's always been about quitting this place, so why
pretend?" But we're always smarter when it's up on the wall,
and standing here is part of the notion, but then
there's the afterparty, where every letter makes a sound
and you have to choose one of your selves to be—

Well? What do you do then?
And for how long?

Reacting Calmly & Quickly

The fissure between what we were thinking and not being able to say it
is of little consequence
to next week's hectic, Scotch-taped ideas
that shatter the small vases,
even if we don't know what to do then, beyond dealing with the crisis
on its own terms, a broom maybe,
or punching the shark in the nose. Then we're able
to take our phone numbers with us, so it all turns out
because it's over, and there are people
sitting around the pool again.

There's a series of waterfalls ahead, I've heard, so it's a risk
that's worth taking, waterfalls being so pretty,
though as soon as we think we've a lasting one, the next
causes us to regret it. The cliffs were too small, or we
added a thirteenth floor. That wasn't the paint
we picked out. And we're standing there with the sense
we're in a car underwater, and we might be upside down,
or aligned with the newest way they're just joking
and looking the other way amid optional vegetation.

A film crew will follow you, they promise. And a little
dog. You've a big white smile,
even if the sky is painted in later, or changed to evening,
and there's this sneaking suspicion
we jumped right to the middle of things
and stayed there,
where you saw whatever you think you saw.

It's the same memoir that we put down a few minutes before,
to tend to the lilacs wilted into the bowl on the counter
that just yesterday you saved from a broken vase. And it's the same page,
I'm sure of it, though I don't remember what it says,
I must have been thinking of the lilacs
or the paint.

And there's nothing to do but start over.

In the Class of All Classes That Are Not Members of Themselves

To see the recognizable geometry of things seen,
you are standing once again beside the birdhouse, which is shoulder-high,
and on a silver pole.

Depending on the staging, it's tree first,
or birdhouse.

Or perhaps the spaniel.

And what is that place like,
as the swirl of dust here forms something of a stair
into clouds
that seem formed for the purpose.

Set as a question, you walk along a field track,
simply following it.

You have buildings in your eyes, buildings small
behind the tree
and this swirl of dust here before you.

A familiarity of cases.

The dog, left forefoot forward.
The tall grass bending in large arcs.

Tell me again
how I don't know what love is.

Duly Noted

Every now and then you've simply got to empty it all out,
purge the files, and make for the fences,
or else make the sort of commotion
that makes it seem the fences might be getting made for
and then make a sort of practical turn
back to the singable songs, a little exhilarated from the exertion
and the thought that music is better
in the end, than that little shock when you look down
and see you're the one standing on the X,
which is always possible, even if you don't actually do things.

Well, we all do things. And later, we do things,
and sometimes with each other
or just reporting back to each other, though by then
the message is kind of garbled
and more about what reporting is, than what it really was
getting to the report, or what we were nattering on so about,
and always with a pleasant closing.

We drove down to visit family on Sunday. It was
an off-stage whisper, and all the squirrels stood up in the yard
expecting something more than we were offering,
which says you'll never be alone again,
but only if you blur your eyes a bit
or change the notion.
Notions are so helpful. And sit there long after we're gone
into escapades or sallying forth.
Perhaps there isn't anything more
to get than that. Perhaps then, so anyway,
thank you for your time. Thank you.

I Will Sing the Monster to Sleep, & He Will Need Me

In the realm of wrong answers, someone
always has the radio on.

Someone is eating, and someone
walking about the room, in the dim café
which ends in a distant range of snow-capped mountains.

There are vanishing people
meeting at the diving board off the window sill,
and a cloud pierced by windows.

There are a lot of things you don't get to decide.

At first, the evenings were filled with stories, music,
or both, with a beige floor
shaded here and there with red.

And then the children are walking across the gravel
in the dark. Always small footsteps
in any manner of realms.

And they quiver like the moon.

Let's look for them awhile, and see what we find
beside the intimidating tower at the summit
of the gently rising square.

There will be water in this pool soon.
And we'll know what happiness is.
There's time, and figures

moving among the arches.

We will take some questions now, they'll say.
Please raise your hand.

Harmony in Tone & Color

Perhaps that's all there is,
wings of desire: the girl
in the swing, and what the dead are up to
this year.

And you're out in the water,
and we can't hear you.
I'm sorry we can't hear you.

Pretend, then, that you know how to swim,
and I'm driving the boat.

We don't have to help each other.

And welcome to the boat. *Hello. Welcome.*
It's a party boat, and everyone's here.

What is the right way in?
And why should the water be anything else?

Pretend I'm the first girl
on the boat,
and this whole thing is a boat.

What kind of water then?
What kind of singing in the water?

A Guess Is Spiritual Then, & Will Try to Help You

Two pregnant women are walking together under the portico.
Early summer. In the cool of the evening.
Making a kind of meaning of it.

But let's start simpler. Let's start
with the sidewalk.
Pay no mind to the barking dogs.

Somewhere near the unthinkable beginning,
where grace might come from.

Some light is yellow. Interior gold.
In total, this all sounds like great progress.

Then they start on the journey. We are going,
they say, into the advancing territory
where all probabilities arrive.

Indeed, this is significant progress.
The amnesia of longing.

And we'd all love to get together there,
and share photographs
amid the balloons and folding chairs,

watching the flashlights bobbing in the field.

The Universe Is Incapable
of Disappearance

They keep talking about a road, but there never is a road,
and if there was, it would always be ending,
the way everything is always ending
unless you're of the mind that everything is always some sort of middle,
or some continual beginning
that rises and falls from a never quite completed something
that we're continually waking from
in a kind of polite vagueness.

And then, what of it? I'm wanting something
or you are, and neither of us is saying what it is past the
"I don't do big emotional things," and I almost feel
like saying sorry, if I were the type to say such things,
or to feel that way. And isn't that some sort of world flying past,
how we realized with a start that being anyone is easy,
and that everyone can do it. And what does that leave us,
other than surrounded by pretty green hills?

And the hills keep feeling like this place to get to,
or to talk about getting to,
even when we realize it's just another window
or painting of a window, which continues for as many years
as there are. That almost feels like it,
but it's not it. Because figures are moving out there,
and somehow they got there, maybe without taking it seriously or trying.

"Call when you find work," we say, though we've heard things
will be different then, perhaps, and maybe they really will find work,
and suddenly we'll no longer be the least bit important. I take notes
because the notes were asking for it. I take notes
because they're teaching children to write differently now. The *t*'s
are larger, and the *k*'s look like *R*'s. Okay, then,
but they're still talking about a road, and about how
in the layered world, it's layers, and everyone says *hello*
from the kitchen windows there
in summer, grayed out a bit by the screens.

Fetish of the Former Life

We spent most of the afternoon there,
touring the model homes. There is the wooden house
and the yellow house
and the green house. The sun shining
and the sun shining.

The model homes in an arc
around the cul-de-sac, and with a pond beyond.

The sun across the Pergo.

There is a maze
in the sound of the grass,
and the sound of a bracelet of houses
in the clear air,

and figures in room plus room,
whichever room
one enters,
speaking low.

Welcome to the sky
on the left
and on the right, they say,

and a pond with ducks in the center,
in a row. You can count them like that,
with ease.

A boy on the little dock.
A girl in the grass.

And the figures go round, and the pond
goes round
and the houses go round
and the houses go round
in the sun.

In the Direction of X. In the City of Zero.

Bob and Carol were driving and took a turn, and now they're at a dead end.
This is another of our habits, like hiding for a very long time.
Or passing by unalarmed.

Bob and Carol took a turn into a parking lot.
This is not our real life, they're thinking.
With these caricatures of our wind and parodies of our sun.
Whatever it is, this is not it.

How worried should we be?
And suppose I don't know whether my answer is right?
It's raining on one side of the parking lot and not on the other, for instance.
In fact, it now looks quite squally there.
So things have changed. They're more modern now.
And they drink coffee to keep awake, where *keep* is an infinitive, the object of
     to; and the phrase *to keep* modifies *drink*.

Bob and Carol find themselves in a parking lot, and they hadn't been looking
     for long.
We're new to this, they're thinking.
And why not think some other thing? Where we wanted to be, perhaps.
Harsher, more beautiful things, like ideas that enter too late.

This morning it rained and it did not rain.
This, then, is from your loose life, where the sound of you breathing is the
     season arriving.
It would not do to tell your secret now.

As this is one of those places along the way.
With the evening halfway on, and one road much like another.

Tonight's the Night

Moon behind the palm trees, with the backs of our heads
in the foreground. It's a lovely evening out there,
with the arcade

and guesses, under the story
of the crashing sea, the fortunate couples.
A palm and a beautiful girl.

It's the way I feel. And all my friends.
For players and dreamers, tonight's the night.

Some smearing of your face, then. Some world on a string
all laid out with breeze and sky, as we're looking in,
visualizing ourselves here.

I'll campaign all my life for that.

And we start counting stars,
but then it's years later, and we're still asking
Where did we go? What were we like?

Some moon there on the sand. Quicksilver.
The barkers and colored lights.

And I sincerely hope I make it back in time.
A picture's worth so many words.

Maybe you could help me.

Hit Me with Your Pillow. Knock Me Over with Your Feather.

Well, later they'll say different things about it, of course, but for a bit
it's great to agree on how it's unfolding, isn't it? Or not even to need to agree,
but instead just act according to some agreement,
the terms of which have never been discussed, but seem to be perfectly
    acceptable
to both parties. They'll never let it continue for long like this,
we always say, but we're in the midst of our own continuing
while saying it, and isn't it funny when we overhear them
saying the very same things about whichever city
the news is featuring this week?

I should know what to do by now, but of course I don't.
And how could I? Look at the vocabulary of these clothes,
the fetish of these windows, the narcolepsy
of the trees ... it's certainly a missing conception, isn't it? And the windows
    don't mind,
do they, that we're starting out again at life with very little on.
And the trees seem rather perky this go-through,
so that maybe after all we could discover there really is
something to find on the other side of the hydrangea,
unless someone's already found it,
but even so, maybe they would leave something else behind,
so that even in finding, we might discover a whole new vista
for what looking might mean,
something other than "wasting your heart,"
as the guidebooks all said, but in much more local colorations.

& Generally the Future
Is Uncertain

Into or out of meaning, the shop is full
of the singing of birds.

And the second is a story. A story
of the birds as they sing.

A story of the singing.

I only want
what you're unable to give.

The music of the birds
from the ceiling. The pictures of birds
along the wall.

Anything else
isn't worth wanting. The faces
in the window, perhaps.

The children on the sidewalk. The shop
next to another shop.

Some final point you might ask yourself.
Some question.

The plastic flowers on the stand.
The sun across the flowers.

Little Eden of the Apocalypse

I borrowed the lilies.
I borrowed the turns of this road.

I borrowed that voice to make my voice.
I borrowed that song you're singing.
Do you like it?

Doesn't it look nice in the sunset
with its answering hint of orange?
Of red?

A bit of one picture
moving into this other picture. This
rampant, this story
of all these bodies
all at once.

I'm tired of the needs of people.

The galleried heads of the chambered voices.

We are as wrong as anything, gilding our shoes
and walking home
in the incandescent twilight.

You Can't Say *No* to the Weather

The pleasures of the restaurant. All these floating narratives
we can walk in and out of. Later,
maybe a county fair. And later, the Devil
may care. And the Tilt-A-Whirl. The calliope house.

We liked it but we couldn't say why,
which made us a bit afraid, but also a bit titillated,
as now we had a secret life,
one filled with unexplainable things. The trick
is to make it seem like it really doesn't matter,
like it's merely happening this way.

I'll take some of that lemonade
with six real lemons, then. And I'll have ten dollars
in tickets, please. Easy as pie.

We've said it too many times
and now it's the only thing there is. But isn't that fine too,
in its way? The curve of things
up and around you, the mad rush of air?

They're saying something back behind the courthouse
that might be interesting. Something
about the voices. The way they're waving their arms
and chewing the scenery. In the photographs,
they might be mistaken for statues.

In that way, though, I suppose we all could,
not in the reductive "what it means" way,
but more in the generalized tone of how the world works,
the way the fairground lights fall across our faces
as we're looking up to the little people in the sky
growing ever more luminous and distant.

Acknowledgments

Arch: "Girl Playing with Toy Soldiers," "The Street," "Harmony in Tone & Color," "Reacting Calmly & Quickly;" *Barn Owl Review*: "Three Panels in Praise of Damage Control," "Caution to the Wind;" *Bayou*: "The Way We Live Now;" *Black Warrior Review*: "Watermelon in the Afternoon;" *Bloomsbury Review*: "Fetish for the World Without Memory;" *Caffeine Destiny*: "What & Who & Where & What," "It's Any Move. It's That People Are Places," "More Versions of *It's Real If You Say It Is;*" *Colorado Review*: "Fetish of the Former Life," "When One Has Lived Too Long Among Other People;" *Denver Quarterly*: "I Believe It Merely Strikes You As if You Know It;" *Field*: "I Will Sing the Monster to Sleep, & He Will Need Me," "Keys to Successful Disappearing," "Apostrophe to the Dead," "You Can't Say *No* to the Weather," "& Generally the Future Is Uncertain;" *Green Mountains Review*: "Work for Killing Time;" *Gulf Coast*: "Anecdote of the Little Houses," "The Universe Is Incapable of Disappearance;" *Hotel Amerika*: "In the Direction of X. In the City of Zero.;" *Interim*: "With the Sunset Machine," "Disguised Afternoon" as "This Is About the House, Not the People;" *The Journal*: "A Guess Is Spiritual Then, & Will Try to Help You," "What We're Up Against," "Anecdote of the Disappearances," "In the Class of All Classes That Are Not Members of Themselves;" *LUNA*: "Little Eden of the Apocalypse;" *New American Writing*: "Hit Me with Your Pillow. Knock Me Over with Your Feather.;" */nor*: "Public Afternoon" as "Public Poem," "The Disease of Clocks;" *Phoebe*: "& All Things Repeatingly;" *Pilot Poetry*: "Minneapolis Is a Fine City," "The Danger in Plans;" *PLEIADES*: "Poem for the End of January;" *Third Coast*: "Tonight's the Night;" *West Branch*: "Earth-tone Anecdote," "For All Things Going Eventually," "This in Which Guidebook," "Duly Noted," "Your Golden Ticket"

Thank you to all who read and talked with me about these poems. There are many, but I must single out Kevin Prufer, Wayne Miller, David Dodd Lee, Hadara Bar-Nadav, Jennifer Militello, and G.C. Waldrep. Thank you to Mary Biddinger for selecting this manuscript for publication, to John Ashbery and Dara Wier for their kind words, to Amy Freels for making it look so nice, and to Robin, Natalie, and Eliot, for everything else.

About the Author

John Gallaher is the author of the books of poetry, *Gentlemen in Turbans, Ladies in Cauls* and *The Little Book of Guesses,* winner of the Levis Poetry Prize. He is currently co-editor of *The Laurel Review* and GreenTower Press.

About the Book

Map of the Folded World was designed and typeset by Amy Freels. The typeface, Vendetta, was designed by John Downer for Emigre. It was released in 1999.

Map of the Folded World was printed on 60-pound Glatfelter Offset Natural and bound by McNaughton & Gunn of Saline, Michigan.